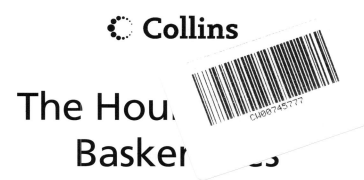

Collins

The Hou...
Basker...

a play by
Carl Miller

adapted from the book by
Arthur Conan Doyle

William Collins' dream of knowledge for all began with the publication of his first book in 1819. A self-educated mill worker, he not only enriched millions of lives, but also founded a flourishing publishing house. Today, staying true to this spirit, Collins books are packed with inspiration, innovation and a practical expertise. They place you at the centre of a world of possibility and give you exactly what you need to explore it.

Collins. Do more.

Published by Collins
An imprint of HarperCollins*Publishers*
77–85 Fulham Palace Road
Hammersmith
London
W6 8JB

Commissioned by Charlie Evans
Design by JPD
Cover design by Paul Manning
Production by Simon Moore
Printed and bound by Martins the Printers

Acknowledgements

Photo credits: Cover, Getty

Browse the complete Collins catalogue at www.collinseducation.com

Contents

Thank you to:

Tony Graham

George Grun

Lucia Grun

Kim Longinotto

Cecily O'Neill

Rebecca Scott

Jonathan Sheldon

Characters

A Group Of Young People

ALI

BROOK

DEVON

MICAH

RAZ

VIC

This group resembles uncannily the group performing the play. They are all on a school trip, camping on a lonely moor. Where the accompanying adults have got to, we will never know.

SHERLOCK HOLMES

JAMES MORTIMER

JOHN WATSON

SIR HENRY BASKERVILLE

JOHN BARRYMORE

ELIZA BARRYMORE

HUGO BASKERVILLE

A MAIDEN

THE HOUND OF THE BASKERVILLES

A COACHMAN

JACK STAPLETON

BERYL STAPLETON

GEORGE SELDEN

LAURA LYONS

Casting

All the 'story' characters (apart perhaps from Holmes) are played by members of the group of young people. 'Naturalistic' casting (in which only a middle-aged white Scottish man can be Dr. Watson, for example) is unnecessary. With a small group, you can combine the parts so that everyone plays two (or even three) roles. A larger group gives opportunities for everyone to have one speaking role but also participate in big group scenes like the story of the Hound.

Depending on the size of your group, you may want to have one Watson, or several. I have indicated with a plus sign (+) the points in the play where a new person might take on the role of Watson. You could think about ways to mark this with a piece of costume, a prop, a physical transformation or other effect.

The whole play should run fluidly, but I have divided it into sections to clarify shifts of location, time or characters.

The Hound of the Baskervilles

Scene 1: *A Tent on the Moor*

Night.

Everyone is inside the tent, in which the light casts ominous shadows.

RAZ	*(reads)* 'Sir Charles lay on his face, his arms out, his fingers dug into the ground, and his features convulsed with –'
BROOK	Convulsed?
MICAH	Distorted.
DEVON	Thrown out of shape.
VIC	Violently disturbed.
ALI	Ssh.
RAZ	'*Convulsed* with some strong emotion to such an extent that I could hardly have sworn to his identity. There was certainly no physical injury of any kind.'
BROOK	So how –
ALI	Ssh.
RAZ	'But one false statement was made by Barrymore at the inquest.'

BROOK	What's an inquest?
MICAH	Where they decide how someone died.
ALI	Who was Barrymore?
DEVON	The butler.
RAZ	Are you listening?
ALI	Sorry.
RAZ	He said –
BROOK	Who said?
MICAH	Barrymore.
VIC	The *butler*.
BROOK	Oh.
RAZ	'He said that there were no traces upon the ground round the body. He did not observe any. But I did – some little distance off, but fresh and clear.'
BROOK	Footprints?
VIC	Footprints.
ALI	A man's or a woman's?
RAZ	'Mr. Holmes, they were the footprints of a gigantic hound!'

One of the group screams.

The group bundles out of the tent.

Scene 2: *Outside the Tent*

The scared are comforted by other group members.

Raz continues to read.

RAZ	'I confess that at these words –'
DEVON	Stop.
ALI	Don't stop.
DEVON	It's scary.
VIC	It's meant to be scary.
DEVON	You're shivering.
MICAH	It's cold.

They look around.

BROOK	What's that?
MICAH	The autumn wind.
VIC	The falling leaves.

Someone sniffs.

BROOK	Damp.
DEVON	Decay.
MICAH	The rain's starting.
RAZ	'That hour of darkness in which the power of evil is exalted.'

DEVON	Don't.

The sound of a long deep mutter, then a rising howl, and then a sad moan in which it dies away.

They listen.

The sound comes again.

BROOK	What's that?
RAZ	I don't know.
MICAH	It's a sound they have on the moor.
ALI	I heard it once before.

The sound comes again.

Silence.

ALI	What do they call this sound?

Pause.

ALI	Tell me.
RAZ	They say it is the cry of the Hound of the Baskervilles.

People react in different ways – some laugh, others whimper.

Someone looks out over the moor.

DEVON	You don't believe it, do you?
VIC	No, no.

Pause.

VIC	And yet –
BROOK	It was one thing to laugh about it back at school.
MICAH	Another to stand out here in the darkness of the moor.
DEVON	And hear such a cry as that.
ALI	I don't think that I'm a coward, but that sound seemed to freeze my blood. Feel my hand.
DEVON	It's cold.
ALI	As a block of marble.
DEVON	I don't think I'll get that cry out of my head.
BROOK	What do we do now?
ALI	Shall we turn back?
MICAH	No. We'll see it through.
RAZ	'If all the fiends of the pit were loose upon the moor – '
DEVON	Don't!

A stranger looms out of the darkness.

Scene 3: *Holmes*

*We shall call the stranger **Holmes**. She or he may be from another class, another school, or even perhaps another time and place entirely.*

HOLMES   Ah, irregulars.

MICAH   Who are you calling irregular?

***Holmes** puts on a distinctive 'Sherlock Holmes' hat.*

ALI   Are you on a school trip too?

***Holmes** takes the book from **Raz**.*

***Holmes** reads, laughing wryly.*

HOLMES   You saw these footprints?

*The group looks at **Holmes** blankly.*

***Holmes** holds out the book.*

*One of the group is pushed forward to become **Mortimer**.*

***Holmes** indicates the place in the book.*

HOLMES   You saw this?

MORTIMER   'As clearly as I see you.'

HOLMES   And you said nothing?

MORTIMER   Er –

*'**Mortimer**' tries to keep up with **Holmes**'s questions, encouraged by the others, becoming increasingly confident.*

MORTIMER	'The marks were some twenty yards from the body, and no-one gave them a thought. I don't suppose I should have done so had I not known the legend.'
HOLMES	There are many sheepdogs on the moor.
MORTIMER	This was no sheepdog.
HOLMES	You say it was large.
MORTIMER	Enormous.
HOLMES	What sort of night was it?
MORTIMER	Damp and raw.
HOLMES	But not actually raining?
MORTIMER	No.
HOLMES	What is the alley like?

Scene 4: *The Yew Alley*

The group maybe set up the crime scene as it is described.

Holmes *examines it minutely.*

MORTIMER	There are two lines of old yew hedge, twelve feet high and impenetrable. The hedge is penetrated at one point by a wicket-gate which leads on to the moor.
HOLMES	Is there any other opening?
MORTIMER	None.
HOLMES	So that to reach the Yew Alley one either has to come down it from the house or enter it by the Moor Gate? Now, tell me – and this is important – the marks which you saw were on the path and not on the grass?
MORTIMER	No marks could show on the grass. They were on the edge of the path on the same side as the Moor Gate.
HOLMES	You interest me exceedingly. Another point. What marks did you see by the wicket-gate?
MORTIMER	None in particular.
HOLMES	Good heavens! Did no-one examine?
MORTIMER	Yes, I examined myself.
HOLMES	And found nothing?
MORTIMER	It was all very confused. Sir Charles had evidently stood there for five or ten minutes.
HOLMES	How do you know that?

MORTIMER	Because the ash had twice dropped from his cigar.
HOLMES	Excellent! This is a colleague, Watson, after our own heart. Watson?

*The group selects its first (or only) '**Watson**' to step forward. (See Casting).*

HOLMES	If I had only been there, Watson. That gravel page upon which I might have read so much has been long ere this smudged by the rain and defaced by the clogs of curious peasants.
MORTIMER	There is a realm in which the most acute and most experienced of detectives is helpless.
HOLMES	You mean that the thing is supernatural?
MORTIMER	I did not positively say so?
HOLMES	No, but you evidently think it.
MORTIMER	Before the terrible event occurred several people had seen a creature upon the moor. They all agreed that it was a huge creature, luminous, ghostly and spectral. I assure you that there is a reign of terror in the district. It is a hardy man who will cross the moor at night.
HOLMES	I see that you have quite gone over to the supernaturalists. If you hold these views, why have you come to consult me at all? You tell me in the same breath that it is useless to investigate Sir Charles's death, and that you desire me to do it.
MORTIMER	I did not say that I desired you to do it.
HOLMES	Then, how can I assist you?

MORTIMER	By advising me as to what I should do with Sir Henry Baskerville.

*One of the group dresses as '**Sir Henry Baskerville**', in a very distinctive tweed suit.*

HOLMES	Sir Henry being the heir?
MORTIMER	On the death of Sir Charles we inquired for this young gentleman and found that he had been farming in Canada.
HOLMES	There is no other claimant, I presume.
MORTIMER	None. There were three brothers, of whom poor Sir Charles was the elder. The second brother, who died young, is the father of this lad Henry. The third, Rodger, made England too hot to hold him, fled to Central America, and died there thirteen years ago of yellow fever. Henry is the last of the Baskervilles.

Scene 5: *221B Baker Street*

Holmes sits in an armchair which has somehow appeared.

HOLMES I have been to Devonshire, Watson.

WATSON In spirit?

HOLMES Exactly. My body has remained in this armchair and has, I regret to observe, consumed in
my absence two large pots of coffee and an
incredible amount of tobacco.

BROOK Where are we now?

MICAH London.

DEVON Number 221B Baker Street.

BROOK Are we?

HOLMES It is an ugly business, an ugly, dangerous
business.

BROOK No. It's a school trip.

HOLMES Here, Watson, is the Ordnance map of this
portion of the moor. My spirit has hovered over
it all day.

Holmes hands *Watson* a map to unroll.

BROOK Why is s/he still Watson?

DEVON I want to be Watson.

+ *Watson* unrolls the map.

HOLMES That is Baskerville Hall in the middle. I fancy

the Yew Alley must stretch along this line, with the moor, as you perceive, upon the right of it. Within a radius of five miles there are, as you see, only a very few scattered dwellings. Then fourteen miles away the great convict prison of Princetown. Between and around these scattered points extends the desolate, lifeless moor. This, then, is the stage upon which tragedy has been played.

WATSON   It must be a wild place.

HOLMES   Yes, the setting is a worthy one. If the devil did desire to have a hand in the affairs of men –

WATSON   Then you are yourself inclining to the supernatural explanation.

HOLMES   The devil's agents may be of flesh and blood, may they not? There are two questions. One is whether any crime has been committed at all; the second is, what is the crime and how was it committed?

Holmes hands *Watson* *a newspaper.*

HOLMES   *The Devon County Chronicle* of May 14th of this year.

Scene 6: *The Death of Sir Charles Baskerville*

Watson reads the newspaper.

WATSON 'Though Sir Charles had resided at Baskerville Hall for a comparatively short period his amiability of character and extreme generosity had won the affection and respect of all who had –'

Holmes gestures impatiently.

WATSON 'In spite of his considerable wealth he was simple in his personal tastes, and his indoor servants at Baskerville Hall consisted of a married couple named Barrymore, the husband acting as butler and the wife as housekeeper.'

MICAH Barrymore!

ALI Ssh.

*Members of the group have become **John** and **Eliza Barrymore**. The group might enact this sequence in the crime scene as **Watson** reads.*

WATSON 'The facts of the case are simple. Sir Charles Baskerville was in the habit every night before going to bed of walking down the famous Yew Alley of Baskerville Hall. On the fourth of May Sir Charles had declared his intention of starting next day for London, and had ordered Barrymore to prepare his luggage. That night he went out as usual for his nocturnal walk, in the course of which he was in the habit of smoking a cigar. He never returned.'

ELIZA At twelve o'clock my husband, finding the hall

door still open, became alarmed, and, lighting a lantern, went in search of his master. The day had been wet, and Sir Charles's footmarks were easily traced down the Alley.

JOHN   My master's footprints altered their character from the time that he passed the moor-gate. He appeared from thence onward to have been walking upon his toes.

Holmes snorts.

WATSON   'No signs of violence were to be discovered upon Sir Charles's person, though the doctor's evidence pointed to an almost incredible facial distortion.'

HOLMES   What do you make of it?

WATSON   It is very bewildering.

HOLMES   That change in the footprints, for example. What do you make of that?

WATSON   The butler said that the man had walked on tiptoe down that portion of the alley.

HOLMES   Why should a man walk on tiptoe down the alley?

WATSON   What then?

HOLMES   He was running, Watson – running desperately, running for his life, running until he burst his heart and fell dead upon his face.

WATSON   Running from what?

HOLMES   There lies our problem. There are indications that the man was crazed with fear before ever he began to run.

WATSON	How can you say that?
HOLMES	Only a man who had lost his wits would have run from the house instead of towards it. Then, again, whom was he waiting for that night, and why was he waiting for him in the Yew Alley rather than in his own house?
WATSON	You think that he was waiting for someone?
HOLMES	The man was elderly and infirm. We can understand his taking an evening stroll, but the ground was damp and the night inclement. Is it natural that he should stand for five or ten minutes, as deduced from the cigar ash? The evidence is that he avoided the moor. That night he waited there. It was the night before he made his departure for London. The thing takes shape, Watson. It becomes coherent.
BROOK	No it doesn't.
HENRY	Quiet. I'm on.

Scene 7: *Sir Henry Baskerville*

Henry greets Holmes and Watson.

HOLMES   Sir Henry Baskerville. The heir.

HENRY   Why yes. Mr. Sherlock Holmes, I understand
that you think out little puzzles, and I have one
which wants more thinking out than I am able
to give it. It was this letter, if you can call it a
letter.

Henry gives Holmes an envelope.

HOLMES   Who knew that you were going to the
Northumberland Hotel?

HENRY   No one could have known.

HOLMES   Someone seems to be very deeply interested in
your movements.

Holmes takes the paper from the envelope and reads.

RAZ   AS

BROOK   YOU

MICAH   VALUE

DEVON   YOUR

VIC   LIFE

ALI   OR

VIC   YOUR

DEVON   REASON

MICAH	KEEP AWAY
BROOK	FROM THE
RAZ	MOOR
WATSON	A single sentence has been formed by the expedient of pasting printed words upon the paper.
HOLMES	The word 'moor' only is written in ink.
HENRY	Now, what in thunder is the meaning of that?
WATSON	There is nothing supernatural about this, at any rate.
HOLMES	It might very well come from someone who was convinced that the business is supernatural.
HENRY	What business? It seems to me that you gentlemen know a great deal more than I do about my own affairs.
HOLMES	Hello! Hello! What's this?

Holmes holds the paper close to his face.

WATSON	Well?
HOLMES	Nothing.

Holmes throws down the paper.

HOLMES	Sir Henry, has anything else of interest happened to you since you have been in London?
HENRY	Well, it depends upon what you think worth reporting.

HOLMES	I think anything out of the ordinary routine of life well worth reporting.
HENRY	I don't know much of British life yet, for I have spent nearly all my time in the States and in Canada. But I hope that to lose one of your boots is not part of the ordinary routine of life over here.
WATSON	You have lost one of your boots?
HENRY	I put them both outside my door last night, and there was only one in the morning.
WATSON	You will find it when you return to the hotel. What is the use of troubling Mr. Holmes with trifles of this kind?
HENRY	The worst of it is that I only bought the pair last night in the Strand, and I have never had them on.
WATSON	On your arrival in London yesterday you went out at once and bought a pair of boots?
HENRY	I did a good deal of shopping. If I am to be squire down there I must dress the part. These out West clothes won't do. I bought brown boots – gave six dollars for them – and had one stolen before ever I had them on my feet. And, now, gentlemen, it seems to me time you gave me a full account of what we are all driving at.
HOLMES	You have in your pocket a manuscript. Early eighteenth century, unless it is a forgery.
HENRY	How can you say that, sir?
HOLMES	You have presented an inch or two of it to my examination all the time that we have been talking. It would be a poor expert who could not give the date of a document within a decade or so. I put that at 1730.

HENRY   The exact date is 1742.

Henry takes the manuscript from his pocket.

HENRY   It is a statement of a certain legend which runs
                   in my family. 'Of the origin of the Hound of the
                   Baskervilles…'

Holmes sighs.

HENRY   Of course, I've heard of the hound ever since I
                   was in the nursery. It's the pet story of the
                   family, though I never thought of taking it
                   seriously before. But as to my uncle's death –
                   you don't seem quite to have made up your
                   mind whether it's a case for a policeman or a
                   clergyman.

HOLMES   The practical point which we now have to
                   decide, Sir Henry, is whether it is or is not
                   advisable for you to go to Baskerville Hall.

HENRY   Why should I not go?

WATSON   There seems to be danger.

HENRY   Do you mean danger from this family legend or
                   do you mean danger from human beings?

HOLMES   Well, that is what we have to find out.

HENRY   Whichever it is, my answer is fixed. There is no
                   devil in hell, Mr. Holmes, and there is no man
                   upon earth who can prevent me from going to
                   the home of my own people.

HOLMES   I am of one mind with you. There is only one
                   provision which I must make. You certainly
                   must not go alone. You must take with you
                   someone, a trusty man, who will be always by
                   your side.

24

HENRY	Is it possible that you could come yourself, Mr. Holmes?
HOLMES	It is impossible for me to be absent from London for an indefinite time.
HENRY	Whom would you recommend, then?

Holmes lays his hand upon Watson's arm.

HOLMES	If my friend would undertake it there is no man who is better worth having at your side when you are in a tight place.

Henry wrings Watson's hand heartily.

HENRY	Well, now, that is real kind of you, Dr. Watson. If you will come down to Baskerville Hall and see me through I'll never forget it.
HOLMES	Then tomorrow, unless you hear to the contrary, we shall meet at the ten-thirty train from Paddington.

Henry leaves.

Holmes sits back in his armchair and thinks.

+ *Watson waits.*

BROOK	What's he doing?
MICAH	Thinking.
VIC	Smoking. Ugh.
WATSON	It's what he does. All afternoon and late into the evening. Endeavouring to find some scheme into which all these strange and apparently disconnected episodes can be fitted.

BROOK	Where did that message come from?
MICAH	That's obvious.
ALI	It is?
MICAH	Look.

Micah picks up The Times.

MICAH	*(reads)* 'As you fear such legislation must in the long run keep away wealth from the country, diminish the value of your imports, and lower the general conditions of life –'
BROOK	What does it mean?
MICAH	It doesn't matter. Look. 'As' 'You' 'Value' 'Your' 'Life' –
VIC	It's what the words were cut out of.
DEVON	But the word 'moor' was written.
MICAH	Because he could not find it in print. The other words were all simple and might be found in any issue.
HOLMES	I tell you, Watson, this time we have got a foeman who is worthy of our steel. I'm not easy in my mind about it.
WATSON	About what?
HOLMES	About sending you. It's an ugly business, Watson, an ugly dangerous business, and the more I see of it the less I like it. Yes, my dear fellow, you may laugh, but I give you my word that I shall be very glad to have you back safe and sound in Baker Street once more.

Scene 8: *Paddington Station*

A burst of steam.

A train whistle.

Passengers, *luggage and* **Guards**.

A newspaper placard reads 'NOTTING HILL MURDERER ESCAPES'.

Holmes *briefs +* **Watson**.

HOLMES	I will not bias your mind by suggesting theories or suspicions, Watson. Record and report the facts to me. You have arms, I suppose?
WATSON	Yes, I thought it as well to take them.
HOLMES	Most certainly. Keep your revolver near you night and day, and never relax your precautions.
WATSON	But what –
HOLMES	Hello, my dear fellow, what on earth is the matter?

Henry arrives, furious and carrying an old black boot.

HENRY	Seems to me they are playing me for a sucker in this country! I can take a joke with the best, Mr. Holmes, but they've gone a bit over the mark this time.
HOLMES	Still looking for your boot?
HENRY	Yes, sir.
WATSON	But, surely, you said that it was a new brown boot?

HENRY	So it was, sir. And now it's an old black one.
WATSON	What! You don't mean to say –
HENRY	Last night they took one of my new brown ones, which reappeared under a cabinet after breakfast. During which they have sneaked one of this old black pair from home!

Watson writes.

WATSON	Another item had been added to that constant and apparently purposeless series of small mysteries which had succeeded each other so rapidly.
RAZ	The whole grim story of Sir Charles's death.
MICAH	The receipt of the printed letter.
DEVON	The loss of the new brown boot.
VIC	The loss of the old black boot.
WATSON	And now the return of the new brown boot.
HOLMES	What are you doing Watson?
WATSON	You asked me to record the facts.
HOLMES	I warn you Watson. This case is never for publication.
WATSON	What do you know of the fellow who found the body – this Barrymore?
HENRY	I understand he is the son of the old caretaker, who is dead. So far as I know, he and his wife are a respectable couple.

WATSON	At the same time, so long as there are none of the family at the Hall these people have a mighty fine home and nothing to do. Did Barrymore profit at all by Sir Charles's will?
HENRY	He and his wife had five hundred pounds each.
WATSON	Ha!
HENRY	I hope that you do not look with suspicious eyes upon everyone who received a legacy from my uncle.
HOLMES	Seven hundred and forty thousand pounds, I understand.
WATSON	I had no idea that so gigantic a sum was involved.
HOLMES	I apologise for the indelicacy.
HENRY	We are not so squeamish as you Brits about mentioning money, Mr. Holmes. The total value of the estate was close on to a million.
HOLMES	It is a stake for which a man might well play a desperate game. Supposing that anything happened to you, Sir Henry – you will forgive the unpleasant hypothesis! – who would inherit the estate?
HENRY	There is no other family I know of.

*A **porter** whistles.*

***Henry** and **Watson** board the train.*

HOLMES	I beg, Sir Henry, that from now on you will not go about alone. Some great misfortune will befall you if you do.

WATSON	Would it not be well in the first place to get rid of this Barrymore couple?
HOLMES	By no means. If they are innocent it would be a cruel injustice, and if they are guilty we should be giving up all chance of bringing it home to them.
HENRY	And will I ever see my old boot, Mr. Holmes?
HOLMES	Indeed. It is very interesting.

Holmes waves goodbye as the train noisily disappears.

HOLMES	Bear in mind, Sir Henry, the family legend, and avoid the moor in those hours of darkness when the powers of evil are exalted.

Scene 9: *The Legend*

The group reassembles on the moor.

RAZ	'Avoid the moor in those hours of darkness when the powers of evil are exalted.'
MICAH	Like now.
DEVON	It's creepy.
ALI	It's just a story. Look. The curse of the Baskervilles.

*Ali produces the document **Henry** had in his pocket.*

ALI	'Of the origin of the Hound of the Baskervilles there have been many statements. Know then, that in the time of the Great Rebellion –'
BROOK	What's that?
MICAH	The English Civil War.
BROOK	There was a civil war in England? Fighting?
DEVON	Hundreds of years ago.
MICAH	Three hundred and sixty.
DEVON	This isn't a lesson.
BROOK	I was interested.
ALI	In the time of the Great Rebellion, this Manor of Baskerville was held by Hugo of that name, a most wild, profane, and godless man.
VIC	That's you.

*Someone becomes **Hugo**.*

HUGO	What are you saying?
ALI	There was in him a certain wanton and cruel humour which made his name a byword through the West.
VIC	It *is* you.
ALI	It chanced that this Hugo came to love –
RAZ	If, indeed, so dark a passion may be known under so bright a name.
ALI	Who's telling this story?
RAZ	Came to love the daughter of a yeoman –
MICAH	A farmer who cultivates his own land.
RAZ	Who held lands near the Baskerville estate.

*Someone becomes the **Maiden**.*

MAIDEN	Me.
RAZ	The young maiden, being discreet and of good repute –
VIC	Is that you?
RAZ	Would ever avoid Hugo, for she feared his evil name.
MAIDEN	It *is* me.
RAZ	So it came to pass that one Michaelmas –
MICAH	29th September, St Michael's Day.
RAZ	This Hugo, with five or six of his idle and wicked companions.

VARIOUS VOLUNTEERS	Me!
RAZ	Stole down upon the farm and carried off the maiden.

*A scuffle during which **Hugo** takes something from the **Maiden** (a book, a shoe, perhaps…)*

RAZ	When they had brought her to the Hall the maiden was placed in an upper chamber, while Hugo and his friends sat down to a long carouse –
BROOK	What's a carouse?
VIC	Here.

Vic hands out drinks. Raucousness ensues.

Ali demands attention.

ALI	Now, the poor lass upstairs was like to have her wits turned at the singing and shouting and terrible oaths which came up to her from below, for they say that the words used by Hugo Baskerville, when he was in wine, were such as might blast the man who said them.

Carousing group members try out some historic curses.

RAZ	At last in the stress of her fear she did that which might have daunted the bravest or most active man, for by the aid of the growth of ivy which covered (and still covers) the south wall she came down from under the eaves, and so homeward across the moor.

*The **Maiden** rushes off.*

Cheers from her supporters.

***Hugo** goes beserk, throwing things aside.*

DEVON	Chill out.
VIC	It's only a story.
HUGO	I will this very night render my body and soul to the Powers of Evil if I might but overtake the wench.
BROOK	What's got into you?
HUGO	Put the hounds upon her!
CAROUSERS	The dogs!
HUGO	Saddle my mare! Unkennel the pack! Here!

***Hugo** gathers the **Hounds** (mimed or created by group members) and gives them the scent of whatever he took from the **Maiden**.*

RAZ	And so off, full cry in the moonlight over the moor.

***Hugo**, the **Hounds** and his supporters pursue the **Maiden**.*

BROOK	I don't like this.
MICAH	It's violent.
BROOK	Creepy.
ALI	What happens?

***Raz** picks up the manuscript.*

RAZ	'For some space the revellers stood agape –'
BROOK	*(standing agape)* What's that?
RAZ	'But anon their bemused wits awoke to the nature of the deed which was like to be done upon the moorlands.'
VIC	Yeah. Let's watch.
BROOK	You are disgusting.
RAZ	Wait!

Devon staggers back on, crazed with fear.

RAZ	Have you seen them?

Silence.

ALI	Have you?

Devon nods, then kneels.

BROOK	What is it?
DEVON	I saw the unhappy maiden, with the hounds upon her track. But I have seen more than that, for Hugo Baskerville passed me upon his black mare, and there ran mute behind him such a hound of hell as god forbid should ever be at my heels.
BROOK	Are you on something?
ALI	Quiet!
RAZ	Listen.

The sound of galloping across the moor.

*The **Hounds** form a terrified circle.*

BROOK What's happened to the dogs?

RAZ 'Though known for their valour and their breed, they were whimpering in a cluster at the head of a deep dip or goyal, as we call it, upon the moor.'

*Three of **Hugo's followers** pull the hounds back to reveal three lying figures.*

*The **Maiden** stands, perhaps leaving something to mark where her body lay.*

MAIDEN The moon was shining bright upon the clearing, and there in the centre lay the unhappy maid where she had fallen, dead of fear and of fatigue.

***Hugo** stands, perhaps leaving something of himself there as the **Maiden** did.*

HUGO But it was not the sight of her body, nor yet was it that of the body of Hugo Baskerville lying near her, which raised the hair upon the heads of the daredevil roisterers.

*The Actor who will be the **Hound of the Baskervilles** rises.*

HOUND ACTOR Standing over Hugo, and plucking at his throat, there stood a foul thing, a great, black beast, shaped like a hound, yet larger than any hound that ever mortal eye has rested upon. And even as they looked the thing tore the throat out of Hugo Baskerville.

*The **Hound Actor** moves towards the others.*

They flee in terror.

*The **Hound Actor** takes up the manuscript.*

HOUND ACTOR   'As it turned its blazing eyes and dripping jaws upon them, they shrieked with fear and rode for dear life, still screaming, across the moor. One, it is said, died that very night of what he had seen, and the others were but broken men for the rest of their days.'

*The **Hound Actor** leaves.*

RAZ   Well.

MICAH   It's a fairytale.

RAZ   'Nor can it be denied that many of the Baskerville family have since been unhappy in their deaths, which have been sudden, bloody, and mysterious.'

ALI   'My sons, I counsel you by way of caution to forbear from crossing the moor in those dark hours when the powers of evil are exalted.'

Those who are left look around the dark, deserted moor.

DEVON   This is not an appropriate location for an educational visit.

VIC   I'm not scared.

BROOK   You're not?

VIC   Well, actually –

A loud train whistle.

Scene 10: *The Moor*

Henry and + Watson step off the train.

HENRY   It's like a landscape from a dream.

A Coachman helps them onto a carriage.

Armed Soldiers pass.

HENRY   Why are there soldiers here?

COACHMAN   There's a convict escaped from Princetown, sir.
                   He's been out three days now, and the warders
                   watch every road and every station, but they've
                   had no sight of him yet.

WATSON   Who is he?

COACHMAN   Selden, the Notting Hill murderer.

WATSON   I remember the case well. Holmes took an
                   interest on account of the peculiar ferocity of
                   the crime and the wanton brutality which had
                   marked all the actions of the assassin.

Pause.

HENRY   Look. The moor.

WATSON   We have left the fertile country behind and
                   beneath us.

HENRY   What are those?

COACHMAN   Cairns, sir.

WATSON   Stones raised in honour of the dead, thousands
                   of years ago.

HENRY	People lived here then? It's desolate.
WATSON	People live here now.

Henry pulls his coat around himself.

WATSON	*(writes)* Somewhere there, on that desolate plain, was lurking this fiendish man –
HENRY	How could Holmes not want you to publish his cases, Dr Watson? You have a vivid style.
WATSON	That's what he objects to. 'This fiendish man hiding in a burrow like a wild beast, his heart full of malignancy against the whole race which had cast him out...'

They travel on in silence.

COACHMAN	Baskerville Hall.

Henry stands and looks.

HENRY	Is that the – ah – the Yew Alley.
COACHMAN	No, sir, that's the other side.
HENRY	It's no wonder my uncle felt as if trouble were coming on him. It's enough to scare any man. I'll have a row of electric lamps up here inside of six months, and you won't know it again.

Eliza and John Barrymore come out.

JOHN	Welcome, Sir Henry. Welcome to Baskerville Hall.

Eliza and John lead Henry and Watson into the Hall.

A great door closes heavily behind them.

Scene 11: *Baskerville Hall*

Henry and + *Watson* warm themselves by the fire.

Eliza and *John* hover.

HENRY
: The stained glass, the oak panelling, the portraits upon the walls – it's just as I imagined it. To think that this should be the same hall in which for five hundred years my people have lived.

Watson examines one of the portraits.

WATSON
: 'Hugo Baskerville, painted 1647.'

HENRY
: Ah, the villain who started it all.

JOHN
: You will find hot water in your rooms, sir. My wife and I will be happy, Sir Henry, to stay with you until you have made your fresh arrangements.

HENRY
: Do you mean that your wife and you wish to leave?

JOHN
: Only when it is quite convenient to you, sir.

HENRY
: But your family have been with us for several generations, have they not?

JOHN
: To tell the truth, sir, I fear that we shall never again be easy in our minds at Baskerville Hall.

HENRY
: But what do you intend to do?

JOHN
: I have no doubt, sir, that we shall succeed in establishing ourselves in some business. Sir Charles's generosity has given us the means to do so. And now, sir, perhaps I had best show you to your rooms.

*John leads **Henry** and **Watson** by candlelight through the house.*

HENRY　　　　　I don't wonder that my uncle got a little jumpy if he lived all alone in such a house as this.

*John silently indicates **Watson**'s room.*

HENRY　　　　　Perhaps things may seem more cheerful in the morning.

*John leads **Henry** away.*

***Watson** looks out.*

A clock strikes far off.

Trees moan and swing in the wind.

Silence.

Then the sob of a woman, a muffled, strangling gasp of uncontrollable sorrow.

Scene 12: *Morning*

Morning breaks.

The group approaches the Hall.

DEVON	That house is spooky.
VIC	It's not so bad in daylight.
DEVON	I'm not going inside.
VIC	*He's* there.
BROOK	Who?
MICAH	The butler. Barrymore.
DEVON	Hide!

*The group hide as **Eliza** and **John** come out of the Hall.*

Eliza and John look around anxiously.

*Henry, in new clothes, and + **Watson** come out of the Hall.*

John and Eliza stop, guiltily.

*Eliza rubs her eyes. **Watson** looks at her.*

JOHN	Sir?
WATSON	I would like to take a look at the Moor this morning.
HENRY	You will forgive me if I stay here. There are numerous papers Barrymore wants examining.

Eliza and John head inside.

HENRY	Mrs. Barrymore? I have placed some of my old clothes aside. I shan't need my American outfits here. Will you be able to find deserving recipients?

Eliza nods and scurries inside, followed by John.

HENRY	What do you make of her?
WATSON	Some deep sorrow gnaws ever at her heart. Sometimes I wonder if she has a guilty memory which haunts her, and sometimes I suspect Barrymore of being a domestic tyrant.
HENRY	I have no fears in sunlight, doctor. Bring me news of any of neighbours you meet.

Henry goes into the Hall and Watson sets off to the Moor.

The group emerge.

MICAH	Barrymore was the last to see Sir Charles alive.
BROOK	Why would he want to kill Baskerville?
DEVON	Or send the cut-out note?
MICAH	To warn him away.
VIC	Maybe he's on his side?
BROOK	Whose side?
RAZ	'Is he the agent of others, or has he some sinister design of his own?'
DEVON	Will you stop doing that!
JACK	*(off)* Doctor Watson!

Scene 13: *Brother and Sister*

Jack Stapleton, *carrying a butterfly net, rushes to intercept +* **Watson** *on the Moor.*

Jack	Excuse my presumption. Here on the moor we are homely folk and do not wait for formal introductions. I am Stapleton, of Merripit House.

Jack and **Watson** *shake hands.*

Jack	I trust that Sir Henry is none the worse for his journey?
Watson	He is very well, thank you.
Jack	We were all rather afraid that after the sad death of Sir Charles the new baronet might refuse to live here. Of course you know the legend of the fiend dog which haunts the family?
Watson	I have heard it.
Jack	It is extraordinary how credulous the peasants are about here! Any number of them are ready to swear that they have seen such a creature upon the moor. The story took a great hold upon the imagination of Sir Charles. His nerves were so worked up that the appearance of any dog might have had a fatal effect upon his diseased heart.
Watson	You think, then, that some dog pursued Sir Charles, and that he died of fright in consequence?
Jack	Have you any better explanation?

WATSON	I have not come to any conclusion.
JACK	Has Mr. Sherlock Holmes?

Pause.

JACK	It is useless for us to pretend that we do not know you, Dr. Watson. If you are here, then it follows that Mr. Sherlock Holmes is interesting himself in the matter, and I am naturally curious to know what view he may take.
WATSON	I am afraid that I cannot answer that question.
JACK	May I ask if he is going to honour us with a visit himself?
WATSON	He cannot leave town at present. He has other cases which engage his attention.
JACK	What a pity! He might throw some light on that which is so dark to us. But as to your own researches, if there is any possible way in which I can be of service to you I trust that you will command me.
WATSON	I assure you that I am simply here upon a visit to my friend, Sir Henry.
JACK	You are perfectly right to be wary and discreet. I promise you that I will not mention the matter again. Perhaps you will spare an hour that I may have the pleasure of introducing you to my sister. We live just along the moor-path.

*Jack indicates the way to **Watson**.*

JACK	You never tire of the moor. You cannot think the wonderful secrets which it contains. It is so vast, and so barren, and so mysterious.

WATSON	You know it well, then?
JACK	I have only been here two years. The residents would call me a newcomer. We came shortly after Sir Charles settled. Look at the hillside yonder. What do you make of those grey circular rings of stone?
WATSON	What are they? Sheep-pens?
JACK	No, they are the homes of our worthy ancestors. Prehistoric man lived thickly on the moor. He grazed his cattle on these slopes, and he learned to dig for tin when the bronze sword began to supersede the stone axe. You can even see his hearth and his couch if you have the curiosity to go inside one of those stone wigwams.
WATSON	Perhaps another day.
JACK	And that great plain to the north. Do you observe anything remarkable about that?
WATSON	It would be a rare place for a gallop.
JACK	The thought has cost several their lives before now. That is the great Grimpen Mire. A false step yonder means death to man or beast. Only yesterday I saw one of the moor ponies wander into it. He never came out. Even in dry seasons it is a danger to cross it, but after these autumn rains it is an awful place.

A dreadful cry echoes over the Moor.

| JACK | Another of those miserable ponies. The mire has him. They get in the way of going there in the dry weather, and never know the difference until the mire has them in its clutches. It's a bad place, the great Grimpen Mire. |

46

WATSON	Why should you wish to go into so horrible a place?
JACK	That is where the rare plants and the butterflies are, if you have the wit to reach them.
WATSON	I shall try my luck some day.
JACK	For God's sake put such an idea out of your mind! Your blood would be upon my head. I assure you that there would not be the least chance of your coming back alive. It is only by remembering certain complex landmarks that I am able to do it.

A long, low moan sweeps over the Moor, swells into a deep roar, and then sinks back into a melancholy, throbbing murmur.

JACK	The peasants say it is the Hound of the Baskervilles calling for its prey. I've heard it once or twice before, but never quite so loud.
WATSON	You are an educated man. You don't believe such nonsense as that?
JACK	It's the mud settling, or the water rising, or something.
WATSON	No, no, that was a living voice.
JACK	Well, perhaps it was. You will find some very singular points about the moor, Dr. Watson. Oh, excuse me an instant! That butterfly is surely Cyclopides.

Jack rushes off in pursuit of a butterfly.

Watson looks around.

A pair of ravens croak loudly.

Beryl Stapleton rushes up to Watson.

WATSON	Is it Miss Stapleton? You do not resemble your brother I must say. He is –
BERYL	Go back! Go straight back to London, instantly.

Watson stares at Beryl.

WATSON	Why should I go back?
BERYL	I cannot explain. But for God's sake do what I ask you. Go back and never set foot upon the moor again.
WATSON	But I have only just come.
BERYL	Man, man! Can you not tell when a warning is for your own good? Go back to London! Start tonight! Get away from this place at all costs! Would you mind getting that orchid for me among the mares-tails yonder?

Jack hurries back to Beryl and Watson.

JACK	Hello, sister!
BERYL	We are very rich in orchids on the moor, though, of course, you are rather late to see the beauties of the place. Jack, you are very hot.
JACK	Yes, I was chasing a Cyclopides. You have introduced yourselves, I can see.
BERYL	Yes. I was telling Sir Henry that it was rather late for him to see the true beauties of the moor.
JACK	Why, who do you think this is?

BERYL	I imagine that it must be Sir Henry Baskerville.
WATSON	No, no, only a humble commoner, but his friend. My name is Dr. Watson.
BERYL	We have been talking at cross-purposes.
WATSON	This is Sir Henry, approaching us. We seem to have circled back to the hall.

Henry comes up.

HENRY	I saw you had company, doctor.
JACK	Stapleton, of Merripit House across the Moor. And this is my sister.
HENRY	Delighted to meet some neighbours. You will join us for lunch at the Hall?

Henry leads Jack off.

HENRY	Talk is you're a naturalist. Tell me your opinion of this legendary hound. You really believe in the interference of the supernatural in the affairs of men?
JACK	All must be speculation, Sir Henry. Yet in similar cases, where families have suffered from some evil influence –

Beryl checks that Henry and Jack cannot hear.

BERYL	I made a stupid mistake in thinking that you were Sir Henry. Please forget the words I said.
WATSON	I am Sir Henry's friend, and his welfare is a very close concern of mine. Tell me why it was that you were so eager that Sir Henry should return to London.

BERYL	A woman's whim, Dr. Watson. When you know me better you will understand that I cannot always give reasons for what I say or do.
WATSON	Please, please, be frank with me, Miss Stapleton, for ever since I have been here I have been conscious of shadows all round me. Life has become like that great Grimpen Mire, with little green patches everywhere into which one may sink and with no guide to point the track.

Pause.

BERYL	You know the story of the hound?
WATSON	I do not believe in such nonsense.
BERYL	But I do. If you have any influence with Sir Henry, take him away from a place which has always been fatal to his family.

John comes out of the Hall.

BERYL	My brother is very anxious to have the Hall inhabited, for he thinks it is for the good of the poor folk upon the moor. He would be very angry if he knew that I have said anything which might induce Sir Henry to go away. But I have done my duty now and I will say no more.

Beryl hurries past John into the Hall.

Watson looks puzzled.

WATSON	Barrymore.
JOHN	Yes, sir?

50

WATSON	Did you happen to hear someone, a woman I think, sobbing in the night?

Pause.

WATSON	Barrymore?
JOHN	There are only two women in the house, sir. One is the scullery maid, who sleeps in the other wing. The other is my wife, and I can answer for it that the sound could not have come from her. Lunch is served, sir.

Watson *considers, then enters the Hall with* **John***.*

The group gathers.

RAZ	'And yet he lied as he said it.'
VIC	How do you know?
RAZ	*(reads)* 'I met Mrs. Barrymore in the long corridor. Her tell-tale eyes were red and glanced at me from between swollen lids. It was she, then, who wept in the night, and if she did so her husband must know it.'
VIC	Why take the risk of lying?
RAZ	What is he hiding?
MICAH	Why is she crying?
DEVON	Where are you going?
ALI	Inside. Waiting for tonight.
DEVON	In there at night-time? No way.

Scene 14: *A Light in the Night*

Darkness.

The group explore with lights.

BROOK Where is this?

MICAH 'A square balustraded gallery ran round the top of the old hall –'

BROOK Balustraded?

DEVON Ssh!

MICAH 'From this central point two long corridors extended the whole length of the building, from which all the bedrooms opened.'

*+ **Watson** hurries **Henry** into his room.*

WATSON Two or three times I have heard steps in the passage, coming and going in the middle of the night.

HENRY We will sit and wait. Lower the lamp.

***Henry** and **Watson** wait in dim light.*

***Watson** writes.*

WATSON 'It was incredible how slowly the hours crawled by –'

***Henry** indicates for silence.*

A clock strikes two.

WATSON	*(writes)* 'We had almost given up in despair –'

Henry and Watson start up.

A creak of a step.

Henry and Watson listen.

They take off their footwear.

The creaking stops.

They go to the passage and look along.

John comes into view, carrying a candle.

Henry and Watson back out of sight.

John goes to a window and looks out into the night.

John holds the candle to the window.

John presses his face against the window.

HENRY	Barrymore!

John springs away from the window.

HENRY	What are you doing here, Barrymore?
JOHN	*(shaking)* Nothing, sir. It was the window, sir. I go round at night to see that they are fastened.
HENRY	No lies! What were you doing at that window?
JOHN	I was doing no harm, sir.
HENRY	Why were you holding a candle to the window?
JOHN	Don't ask me, Sir Henry – don't ask me! It is not my secret, and I cannot tell it.

Watson takes the candle from John.

WATSON   He must have been holding it as a signal. Let us see if there is any answer.

Watson holds the candle to the window as John did.

WATSON   There it is!

JOHN   No, no, sir, it is nothing – nothing at all!

HENRY   Move your light across the window, Watson! See, the other moves also! Now, you rascal, do you deny that it is a signal? Come, speak up! Who is your confederate out yonder, and what is this conspiracy that is going on?

JOHN   It is my business, and not yours. I will not tell.

HENRY   Then you leave my employment right away.

JOHN   Very good, sir. If I must I must.

HENRY   And you go in disgrace. By thunder, you may well be ashamed of yourself. Your family has lived with mine for over a hundred years under this roof, and here I find you deep in some dark plot against me.

ELIZA   No, no, sir; no, not against you!

Eliza emerges from the darkness.

JOHN   We have to go, Eliza. This is the end of it.

ELIZA   It is my doing, Sir Henry – all mine. He has done nothing except for my sake and because I asked him. My unhappy brother is starving on the moor. We cannot let him perish at our very gates. The light is a signal to him that food is

	ready for him, and his light out yonder is to show the spot to which to bring it.
WATSON	Then your brother is –
ELIZA	The escaped convict, sir – Selden, the criminal.
JOHN	That's the truth, sir. I said that it was not my secret and that I could not tell it to you. But now you have heard it, and you will see that if there was a plot it was not against you.
ELIZA	When my brother dragged himself here one night, weary and starving, with the warders hard at his heels, what could we do? We took him in and fed him and cared for him. Then you returned, sir, and my brother thought he would be safer on the moor than anywhere else until the hue and cry was over. We made sure if he was still there by putting a light in the window, and if there was an answer my husband took out some bread and meat to him. Every day we hoped that he was gone, but as long as he was there we could not desert him. That is the whole truth, as I am an honest Christian woman.

John and *Eliza* hold on to each other.

| **HENRY** | We shall talk further about this matter in the morning. |

John and *Eliza* leave.

Henry and *Watson* look out through the window.

| **HENRY** | I wonder he dares shine a light out there. |
| **WATSON** | How far do you think it is? |

HENRY   It cannot be far if Barrymore had to carry out the food to it. And he is waiting, this villain, beside that candle. By thunder, Watson, I am going out to take that man!

Henry rushes off.

Scene 15: *The Man on the Tor*

Members of the group search the moonlit Moor.

MICAH	The light came from round here.
DEVON	I want to be in bed.
VIC	I couldn't sleep now.
DEVON	Why have you got a gun?
MICAH	It's Watson's.
RAZ	'He is said to be a desperate fellow.'
BROOK	Watson?
RAZ	The murderer.

Someone moans with fear and cold.

Henry *and +* **Watson** *clamber up.*

HENRY	I say, Watson, what would Holmes say to this? How about that hour of darkness in which the power of evil is exalted?
DEVON	I wish people would stop saying that.

The sound of a long deep mutter, then a rising howl, and then a sad moan in which it dies away.

They listen.

The sound comes again.

HENRY	What's that?

WATSON	I don't know. It's a sound they have on the moor. I heard it once before.
HENRY	What do they call this sound?
WATSON	Who?
HENRY	The folk on the countryside.
WATSON	Oh they are ignorant people. Why should you mind what they call it?
HENRY	Tell me, Watson.

Pause.

WATSON	They say it is the cry of the Hound of the Baskervilles.

Silence.

*A crazed figure – **Selden** – leaps up and hurls a rock at **Henry** and **Watson**.*

SELDEN	DIE!

***Henry** and **Watson** dive for cover as the rock shatters.*

***Selden** runs into the night.*

***Watson** pulls out his gun.*

ALI	Look.
MICAH	What? He ran that way.
VIC	There, where the moon is.

*Someone points towards the moon – the opposite direction to that taken by **Selden**.*

BROOK	A figure upon the hill.
MICAH	Upon the tor.
RAZ	See.
DEVON	Yes.
RAZ	'As if brooding over that enormous wilderness of peat and granite.'
MICAH	The very spirit of this terrible place.
BROOK	It's not the convict.
VIC	He ran the other way.
ALI	This is someone else.

Henry and *Watson* stagger back, panting.

Watson cries out when he notices the figure on the tor and grabs *Henry*'s arm.

WATSON	Who was that?
HENRY	A warder, no doubt. The moor has been thick with them since this fellow escaped. Back to the Hall.

Henry and *Watson* head back.

Watson keeps peering for another sight of the figure.

RAZ	'There was the sharp pinnacle of granite still cutting the lower edge of the moon, but its peak bore no trace of that silent and motionless figure.'

Scene 16: *L.L.*

The group compare notes.

ALI   So. What's your theory?

BROOK   I'm completely confused.

RAZ   'A dull and foggy day with a drizzle of rain.'

DEVON   That's not helping.

RAZ   'The house is banked in with rolling clouds, which rise now and then to show the dreary curves of the moor, with thin, silver veins upon the sides of the hills, and the distant boulders gleaming where the light strikes upon their wet faces.'

DEVON   I said stop.

RAZ   'It is melancholy outside and in.'

VIC   I feel –

ALI   What?

VIC   A weight at my heart.

RAZ   A feeling of impending danger.

BROOK   What danger?

VIC   That's what's terrible. I can't define it.

ALI   Sir Charles's death –

RAZ   Exactly as the legend predicted.

ALI   The strange creature on the moor.

MICAH   It's a myth.

DEVON	I've heard it.
ALI	Twice.
MICAH	It's a figment.
DEVON	A figment that leaves footprints?
MICAH	Where does it hide? Where does it get its food? Why does no one see it by day?
ALI	And the letter.
DEVON	That was real.
VIC	But was it the work of a friend?
RAZ	Or an enemy?
VIC	And where is that friend –
RAZ	Or enemy –
VIC	Now?

+ *Watson looks out with binoculars.*

WATSON	Could he be the stranger last night upon the tor?

*Henry enters with **Eliza** and **John**.*

HENRY	The Barrymores consider that they have a grievance.
JOHN	I was very much surprised when I heard you two gentlemen come back this morning and learned that you had been chasing Selden. The poor fellow has enough to fight against without my putting more upon his track.

HENRY	If you had told us of your own free will it would have been a different thing. You only told us, or rather your wife only told us, when it was forced from you.
ELIZA	I didn't think you would have taken advantage of it, Sir Henry – indeed I didn't.
WATSON	The man is a public danger.
JOHN	He'll break into no house, sir. I give you my solemn word upon that.
ELIZA	For God's sake, sir, I beg of you not to let the police know that he is still on the moor. They have given up the chase there, and he can lie quiet until the ship is ready for him.
JOHN	To commit a crime would be to show where he was hiding.
HENRY	That is true. I guess we are aiding and abetting a felony, Watson? But, after what we have heard I don't feel as if I could give the man up, so there is an end of it. All right, you can go.
ELIZA	God bless you, sir, and thank you from my heart!
JOHN	It would have killed my poor wife had he been taken again.

Eliza and *John* are about to leave but turn back.

JOHN	You've been so kind to us, sir, that I should like to do the best I can for you in return. I know something, Sir Henry, and perhaps I should have said it before, but it was long after the inquest that I found it out. It's about poor Sir Charles's death.

Henry and *Watson* start.

HENRY	Do you know how he died?
JOHN	No, sir, I don't know that.
HENRY	What then?
JOHN	I know why he was at the gate at that hour. It was to meet a woman.
HENRY	To meet a woman! He?
JOHN	Yes, sir.
WATSON	And the woman's name?
JOHN	I can't give you the name, sir, but her initials were L. L.

Pause.

JOHN	Your uncle had a letter that morning. It was from Coombe Tracey, and it was addressed in a woman's hand.
HENRY	Well?
ELIZA	When I was cleaning out Sir Charles's study – it had never been touched since his death – I found the ashes of a burned letter in the back of the grate. One little slip, the end of a page, hung together.

Eliza looks to *John*. *He nods.*

ELIZA	It said: 'Please, please, as you are a gentleman, burn this letter, and be at the gate by ten o'clock.' Beneath it were signed the initials L. L.

WATSON	Have you got that slip?
ELIZA	No, sir, it crumbled all to bits after I moved it.
HENRY	I cannot understand, Barrymore, how you came to conceal this important information.
ELIZA	It's well to go carefully when there's a lady in the case.
HENRY	You thought it might injure his reputation?
JOHN	Well, sir, I thought no good could come of it. But now you have been kind to us, and I feel as if it would be treating you unfairly not to tell you all that we know about the matter.
HENRY	Very good, Barrymore.

Henry leaves.

WATSON	Will you need to leave more food tonight?
JOHN	He has enough for now. Unless the other man has taken it.

Watson stares at John.

WATSON	You know that there is another man then?
JOHN	Yes, sir, there is another man upon the moor.
WATSON	Have you seen him?
JOHN	No, sir.
WATSON	How do you know of him then?
JOHN	Selden told me of him, sir. He's in hiding, too, but he's not a convict as far as I can make out.

ELIZA	I don't like it. I tell you straight, sirs, that I don't like it. It's all these goings-on. Look at Sir Charles's death! That was bad enough. Look at the noises on the moor at night. There's not a man would cross it after sundown if he was paid for it. Look at this stranger hiding out yonder, and watching and waiting! What's he waiting for? What does it mean?
JOHN	It means no good to anyone of the name of Baskerville.
WATSON	But about this stranger. Where did your brother say that he lived?
JOHN	Among the old houses on the hillside – the stone huts where the old folk used to live.
ELIZA	He has got a lad who works for him and brings him all he needs.
WATSON	It is a wild enough day indoors.
JOHN	Sir?
WATSON	What must it be like in a stone hut upon the moor?
JOHN	Is that all, sir?
WATSON	What passion of hatred can it be which leads a man to lurk in such a place at such a time! There, in that hut upon the moor, seems to lie the very centre of that problem which has vexed me so sorely.

Watson shakes his head.

The wind howls.

Scene 17: *The Stone Hut*

Group members examine the Neolithic huts.

MICAH	The homes of our worthy ancestors.
VIC	You can even see his hearth and his couch if you have the curiosity to go inside.
DEVON	No sound.
BROOK	No movement.

Raz points.

RAZ	One great grey bird.
MICAH	A gull.
DEVON	Or curlew.
RAZ	'He and I seemed to be the only living things between the huge arch of the sky and the desert beneath it.'
DEVON	Do you enjoy that?
VIC	The old stone huts.
ALI	This one's got enough roof for shelter.

*+ **Watson** appears.*

WATSON	This must be the burrow where the stranger lurks.

***Watson** warily approaches the hut.*

He listens.

He takes out a gun.

He walks swiftly to the entrance of the hut and looks in.

ALI	Blankets.
BROOK	Ashes of a fire.
RAZ	Cooking utensils.
VIC	A bucket half-full of water.
DEVON	A litter of empty tins.
MICAH	A pannikin.
BROOK	What?
MICAH	A small pan or cup.
VIC	A half-full bottle of spirits.
MICAH	A small cloth bundle containing a loaf of bread, a tinned tongue, and two tins of preserved peaches.
DEVON	How do you know –
ALI	A sheet of paper with writing upon it.

Watson *picks up the paper.*

WATSON	*(reads)* 'Dr. Watson is searching the moor.'
DEVON	Oh oh.

Pause.

'An unseen force, a fine net drawn round us
with infinite skill and delicacy, holding us so
lightly that it was only at some supreme
moment that one realized that one was indeed
entangled in its meshes.'

Someone makes the clink of a boot on stone.

DEVON   Hide!

*The group members leave **Watson** alone.*

Footsteps continue.

***Watson** shrinks back into the shadows.*

The footsteps stop.

***Watson** cocks his pistol.*

A shadow falls across the opening of the hut.

Scene 18: *The Murderer*

HOLMES	It is a lovely evening, my dear Watson. I really think that you will be more comfortable outside than in.

Holmes comes into view.

WATSON	Holmes! Holmes!
HOLMES	Come out, and please be careful with the revolver.

Watson comes out of the hut.

WATSON	I never was more glad to see anyone in my life.
HOLMES	Or more astonished, eh?
WATSON	Well, I must confess to it.
HOLMES	So you actually thought that I was the criminal?
WATSON	I thought that you were in Baker Street.
HOLMES	That was what I wished you to think.
WATSON	Then you use me, and yet do not trust me!
HOLMES	Had I been with Sir Henry and you, my presence would have warned our very formidable opponents to be on their guard.
WATSON	And can you tell me what we are dealing with?
HOLMES	It is murder, Watson – refined, cold-blooded, deliberate murder. My nets are closing upon him, even as his are upon Sir Henry, and with

	your help he is already almost at my mercy. There is but one danger which can threaten us. It is that he should strike before we are ready to do so.
WATSON	Who?
HOLMES	The intimate friend of Mrs. Laura Lyons of Coombe Tracey.
WATSON	Is that the L.L. who wrote to Sir Charles the night he died?
HOLMES	The very same. It must be our first duty to see her – both of us – tomorrow. But now Watson, you are away from your charge overlong. Your place should be at Baskerville Hall.
WATSON	But who is our enemy?
HOLMES	You have seen the portrait of the wicked Hugo, who started the Hound of the Baskervilles.
WATSON	I am not likely to forget him. But he died centuries ago.
HOLMES	Describe the picture.
WATSON	A broad plumed hat, curling love-locks, a white lace collar –
HOLMES	The face, Watson, the face!
WATSON	It is not a brutal countenance, but it is prim, hard, and stern, with a firm-set, thin-lipped mouth, and a coldly intolerant eye.
HOLMES	Is it like anyone you know?
WATSON	There is something of Sir Henry about the jaw.
HOLMES	Just a suggestion, perhaps. Forget the hat, the hair. See the face before you.

Watson considers.

WATSON	Good heavens!
HOLMES	Yes.
WATSON	Stapleton?
HOLMES	The fellow is a Baskerville – that is evident. Although for many years he posed as one Vandaleur, a noted expert on moths and butterflies. He shares the name of his dead father, Rodger Baskerville.
WATSON	Sir Charles's brother in South America?
HOLMES	Where he fled with a sinister reputation and – as we know – died. What no-one knew was that he had a son.
WATSON	Who is in line to inherit.
HOLMES	Yes, Watson. Vandaleur came here to Devonshire and became Stapleton when he discovered that only two lives intervened between him and a valuable estate. Sir Charles is dead.
WATSON	And Sir Henry –
HOLMES	Is in mortal peril. Another day – two at the most – and I have my case complete, but until then guard your charge as closely as ever a fond mother watched her ailing child. Your mission today has justified itself, and yet I could almost wish that you had not left his side. Hark!

A terrible scream – a prolonged yell of horror and anguish – bursts out of the silence.

Holmes *leaps to his feet.*

WATSON	Oh, my God! What is it? What does it mean?
HOLMES	Hush! Hush! Where is it? Where is it, Watson?
WATSON	There, I think.
HOLMES	No, there!

The cry sounds again, louder and nearer.

Another sound mingles with it, a deep muttered rumble, rising and falling.

| HOLMES | The hound! Come, Watson, come! Great heavens, if we are too late! |

A despairing yell –

And then a dull, heavy thud.

Silence.

Holmes *puts his hand to his head.*

HOLMES	He has beaten us, Watson. We are too late.
WATSON	No, no, surely not!
HOLMES	Fool that I was to hold my hand. And you, Watson, see what comes of abandoning your charge!

Scene 19: *Death on the Moor*

Members of the group enter into the gloom with torches.

MICAH	Can you see anything?
BROOK	Nothing.
ALI	What is that?

*Torches shine onto a fallen body dressed in **Henry**'s distinctive tweed suit.*

VIC	Ugh.
DEVON	Blood.
RAZ	'The ghastly pool widened slowly from the crushed skull of the victim.'

Holmes *and* **Watson** *rush on.*

Holmes *strikes a match and lays his hand upon the body.*

He looks at his fingers – they are matted with blood.

The match flickers and goes out.

WATSON	The brute! The brute! Oh Holmes, I shall never forgive myself for having left him to his fate.
HOLMES	I am more to blame than you, Watson. In order to have my case well rounded and complete, I have thrown away the life of my client. But how could I know that he would risk his life alone upon the moor in the face of all my warnings?
WATSON	That we should have heard his screams and yet have been unable to save him!

HOLMES	Uncle and nephew have been murdered – the one frightened to death by the very sight of a beast which he thought to be supernatural, the other driven off that cliff in his wild flight to escape from it.
WATSON	We must seize Stapleton at once.
HOLMES	We have to prove the connection between the man and the beast. It is not what we know, but what we can prove. If we make one false move the villain may escape us yet.
WATSON	What can we do?
HOLMES	Tonight we can only perform the last offices to our poor friend.

Holmes bends over the body.

WATSON	We must send for help, Holmes! We cannot carry him all the way to the Hall.

Holmes cries out and laughs.

WATSON	Good heavens, are you mad?

Holmes wrings Watson's hand.

HOLMES	A beard! A beard! The man has a beard!
WATSON	A beard?
HOLMES	It is not the baronet – it is – why, it is my neighbour, the convict!

Holmes and Watson turn over the body to reveal Selden's face.

WATSON	Sir Henry handed his old wardrobe to the Barrymores. They must have passed it on in order to help Selden in his escape.

HOLMES	Then the clothes have been the poor devil's death. The hound had already been set on Sir Henry's scent.
WATSON	But how?
HOLMES	The boots, Watson. Or rather, the boot.
WATSON	That's why they were stolen?
HOLMES	The first boot stolen was a new one, and therefore useless for our killer's purpose. He therefore obtained another – a most instructive incident since it proved conclusively to my mind that we were dealing with a real hound. But what's this! It's the man himself, by all that's wonderful and audacious! Not a word to show your suspicions – not a word, or my plans crumble to the ground.

Jack enters.

JACK	Why, Dr Watson, that's not you, is it? You are the last man that I should have expected to see out on the moor at this time of night. But, dear me, what's this? Somebody hurt? Not – don't tell me that it is our friend Sir Henry!

Jack stoops over the body.

JACK	Who – who's this?
WATSON	It is Selden, the man who escaped from Princetown.

Pause.

JACK	Dear me! What a very shocking affair! How did he die?

WATSON	Anxiety and exposure had driven him off his head. He has rushed about the moor in a crazy state and eventually fallen over here and broken his neck.
JACK	What do you think about it, Mr. Sherlock Holmes?
HOLMES	You are quick at identification.
JACK	We have been expecting you in these parts since Dr. Watson came down. You are in time to see a tragedy.
HOLMES	Yes, indeed. I will take an unpleasant remembrance back to London with me tomorrow.
JACK	Oh, you return tomorrow?
HOLMES	That is my intention.
JACK	I hope your visit has cast some light upon those occurrences which have puzzled us? Did you hear anything else besides this man's cry?
HOLMES	No, did you?
JACK	No.

Pause.

JACK	You know the stories that the peasants tell about a phantom hound, and so on.
HOLMES	An investigator needs facts, and not legends or rumours. It has not been a satisfactory case.
JACK	I would suggest carrying this poor fellow to my house, but it would give my sister such a fright. If we put something over his face he will be safe until morning. But you will come back with me to Merripit?
WATSON	We should return to Sir Henry.

JACK	Yes. That was what brought me out. I was uneasy about Sir Henry.
HOLMES	Why about Sir Henry in particular?
JACK	Because I had suggested that he should come over to us. When he did not come I was surprised, and I naturally became alarmed for his safety when I heard cries upon the moor. You will all three join my sister and I for dinner tomorrow night, I hope?
WATSON	Very kind.
JACK	Goodnight gentlemen.
HOLMES	Goodnight.

Jack leaves.

HOLMES	I told you in London, Watson, and I tell you now again, that we have never had a foeman more worthy of our steel.
WATSON	Why should we not arrest him at once?
HOLMES	We could prove nothing against him.
WATSON	Surely we have a case.
HOLMES	Not a shadow of one, but is worth our while to run any risk in order to establish one.
WATSON	And how do you propose to do so?
HOLMES	I have great hopes of Mrs. Laura Lyons.

Holmes leads Watson off.

HOLMES	Say nothing of the hound to Sir Henry. He will have a better nerve for the ordeal which he will have to undergo tomorrow.

Scene 20: *Baiting the Trap*

BROOK   So there is a dog.

DEVON   I always thought there was.

MICAH   Ever since the boots.

RAZ   'A most instructive incident.'

BROOK   But why did Stapleton send the letter? Why warn Sir Henry?

VIC   Did he send the letter?

ALI   But then –

Henry, Holmes and Watson enter.

HENRY   I had been expecting these events would bring you down at last, Mr. Holmes.

HOLMES   We are engaged to dine with your friends the Stapletons tonight.

HENRY   They are very hospitable people.

HOLMES   But I fear that Watson and I must go to London.

HENRY   To London? I hoped that you were going to see me through this business. The Hall and the moor are not very pleasant places when one is alone.

HOLMES   My dear fellow, you must trust me implicitly and do exactly what I tell you. You can tell your friends that we should have been happy to have come with you, but that urgent business required us to be in town. Will you remember to give them that message?

HENRY	If you insist upon it.
HOLMES	There is no alternative, I assure you.
HENRY	I have a good mind to go to London with you. Why should I stay here alone?
HOLMES	Because it is your post of duty. Because you gave me your word that you would do as you were told, and I tell you to stay.
HENRY	All right, then, I'll stay.
HOLMES	One more direction! I wish you to drive to Merripit House. Send back your trap, however, and let them know that you intend to walk home.
HENRY	To walk across the moor?
HOLMES	Yes.
HENRY	But that is the very thing which you have so often cautioned me not to do.
HOLMES	If I had not every confidence in your nerve and courage I would not suggest it, but it is essential that you should do it.
HENRY	Then I will.
HOLMES	And as you value your life do not go across the moor in any direction save along the straight path which leads from Merripit House to the Grimpen Road, and is your natural way home.
HENRY	I will do just what you say.
HOLMES	Very good.

Henry leaves.

HOLMES	Now, Watson, I think that we cannot employ our time better than by calling upon Mrs. Laura Lyons.

Scene 21: *A false scent*

Some group members wait at the station, bags packed.

VIC We're getting the train home.

DEVON I'm not camping out on a moor with a mad dog.

BROOK Not any more.

VIC Not any moor. Get it?

ALI The hound's not got your scent.

MICAH Unless we gave it one of your trainers.

DEVON Stop it!

***Holmes** and + **Watson** arrive. **Holmes** selects one of the group heading home.*

HOLMES You!

PASSENGER Me?

HOLMES You are taking this train to town? The moment you arrive in London you will send a wire to Mr. Stapleton of Merripit House in my name, to say that I am sorry not to be dining with him and his sister this evening.

PASSENGER Yes, sir.

A train sounds.

***Holmes** and **Watson** leave.*

PASSENGER Is that my whole part? 'Yes sir'?

MICAH	Don't you see?
BROOK	What?
MICAH	He's letting the Stapletons think he's gone to London so they'll be lulled into a false sense of security.

*Group members hurry off after **Holmes** and **Watson**.*

BROOK	Where are you going?
MICAH	Mrs. Laura Lyons's.

Scene 22: *Mrs. Laura Lyons*

Holmes and + Watson greet Laura Lyons. Group members crowd round.

LAURA	I am Mrs. Laura Lyons.
WATSON	You are a typist.
LAURA	I have a small typewriting business.
RAZ	*(reads)* 'The first impression left by Mrs. Lyons was one of extreme beauty.'
VIC	Ooh.
RAZ	'Her eyes and hair were of the same rich hazel colour, and her cheeks, though considerably freckled, were flushed with the exquisite bloom of the brunette, the dainty pink which lurks at the heart of the sulphur rose.'
VIC	Calm down.
RAZ	'But there was something subtly wrong with the face, some coarseness of expression, some hardness, perhaps, of eye, some looseness of lip which marred its perfect beauty.'

Whoever plays Laura shoos the others out.

WATSON	We have come here to see you about the late Sir Charles Baskerville.
LAURA	What can I tell you about him?
WATSON	You knew him, did you not?
LAURA	I owe a great deal to his kindness. If it were not for him and some other kind hearts I might have starved after my unfortunate marriage.

WATSON	Did you correspond with Sir Charles?
LAURA	I certainly wrote to him once or twice to acknowledge his delicacy and his generosity. What is the object of these questions?
WATSON	You wrote to Sir Charles asking him to meet you.
LAURA	Really, sir, this is a very extraordinary question.
HOLMES	'Please, please, as you are a gentleman, burn this letter, and be at the gate by ten o'clock.'

Pause.

LAURA	Is there no such thing as a gentleman?
WATSON	You do Sir Charles an injustice. He did burn the letter. But sometimes a letter may be legible even when burned.
LAURA	I have no reason to be ashamed of it. I wished him to help me again, so I asked him to meet me.
HOLMES	At such an hour?
LAURA	I had only just learned that he was going to London next day and might be away for months.
HOLMES	But why a rendezvous in the garden instead of a visit to the house?
LAURA	Do you think a woman could go alone at that hour to a bachelor's house?
HOLMES	Well, what happened when you did get there?
LAURA	I never went.

HOLMES	Mrs. Lyons!
LAURA	No, I swear it to you on all I hold sacred. I never went. Something intervened to prevent my going.
WATSON	What was that?
LAURA	That is a private matter. I cannot tell it.
HOLMES	You have confessed that you asked Sir Charles to be at the gate at ten o'clock. We know that that was the place and hour of his death. You have withheld what the connection is between these events.
LAURA	There is no connection.
HOLMES	I wish to be perfectly frank with you, Mrs. Lyons. We regard this case as one of murder, and the evidence may implicate not only your friend Mr. Stapleton, but his wife as well.
LAURA	His wife!
WATSON	His wife?
HOLMES	The person who has passed for his sister is really his wife.
WATSON	Good heavens Holmes! Are you sure of what you say?
LAURA	His wife!
HOLMES	I repeat that the lady is his wife and not his sister.
WATSON	But why this elaborate deception?
HOLMES	Because he foresaw that she would be very much more useful to him in the character of a free woman.

LAURA	He is not a married man.
HOLMES	When I examined the paper upon which those printed words were fastened I made a close inspection for the water-mark. In doing so I held it within a few inches of my eyes, and was conscious of a faint smell of the scent known as white jessamine. The scent suggested the presence of a lady.
LAURA	Prove it to me! Prove it to me! And if you can do so –

Holmes takes out a photograph.

HOLMES	Here is a photograph of the couple taken in York four years ago. It is endorsed 'Mr. and Mrs. Vandaleur,' but you will have no difficulty in recognizing him, and her also.

Laura examines the photograph.

LAURA	Mr. Holmes, this man had offered me marriage on condition that I could get a divorce from my husband. He has lied to me, the villain, in every conceivable way. One thing I swear to you, and that is that when I wrote the letter I never dreamed of any harm to the old gentleman, who had been my kindest friend.
WATSON	I entirely believe you, madam.
LAURA	Why should I preserve faith with him who never kept any with me? Ask me what you like, and there is nothing which I shall hold back.
WATSON	The sending of this letter was suggested to you by Stapleton?

LAURA	He dictated it – pleading help from Sir Charles for the legal expenses connected with my divorce.
HOLMES	And then after you had sent the letter he dissuaded you from keeping the appointment?
WATSON	And then you heard nothing until you read the reports of the death in the paper?
LAURA	He made me swear to say nothing – said that I should certainly be suspected if the facts came out.
WATSON	But you had your suspicions?

Laura looks down.

LAURA	If he had kept faith with me I should always have done so with him.
HOLMES	I think that on the whole you have had a fortunate escape. You have had him in your power and he knew it, and yet you are alive. We must wish you good morning now, Mrs. Lyons.

Holmes and Watson leave Laura alone.

Scene 23: *Watching and Waiting*

Holmes *is silent.*

+ ***Watson*** *and the group members wait.*

WATSON	One of Sherlock Holmes's defects – if, indeed, one may call it a defect – is that he is exceedingly loath to communicate his full plans to any other person until the instant of their fulfilment.
BROOK	What?
MICAH	He won't tell us what he's plotting.
WATSON	The result is very trying for those who are acting as his agents and assistants.
HOLMES	Come on. *(to **Ali**)* Are you armed?
BROOK	What's the game now?
HOLMES	A waiting game.
DEVON	It's not a very cheerful place.
ALI	I see the lights of a house ahead.
HOLMES	That is Merripit House and the end of our journey. I must request you to walk on tiptoe and not to talk above a whisper.

They all move cautiously towards the house.

HOLMES	This will do. These rocks upon the right make an admirable screen.
DEVON	Wait here?

HOLMES	Get into this hollow. Watson, can you tell the position of the rooms?
WATSON	That is certainly the dining room.
HOLMES	The blinds are up. Creep forward quietly and see what they are doing – but for heaven's sake don't let them know that they are watched.

Watson creeps closer to the house and looks in.

Holmes looks across the moor.

HOLMES	Fog!

Watson returns.

WATSON	There were only two men in the room, Sir Henry and Stapleton. Stapleton was talking with animation, but the baronet looked pale and distrait.
HOLMES	The lady is not there?
WATSON	No.
HOLMES	Where can she be, then?

Holmes indicates the moor.

HOLMES	The fog is moving towards us, Watson.
WATSON	Is that serious?
HOLMES	Very serious, indeed – the one thing upon earth which could have disarranged my plans. In half an hour we won't be able to see our hands in front of us.

Holmes addresses the group members.

HOLMES　　　　　You will move farther back upon higher ground. But not too far. We dare not take the chance of Sir Henry being overtaken before he can reach you.

The group members move off towards the moor.

Henry and Jack appear at a door.

Holmes and Watson watch as Henry sets off, apprehensively, across the moor.

As soon as Henry is out of sight, Jack takes out a key and goes around the house.

HOLMES　　　　　Quick, Watson.

WATSON　　　　　What about the lady?

HOLMES　　　　　What of her?

Watson rushes into the house.

HOLMES　　　　　Watson!

Holmes, furious, follows.

Scene 24: *The Butterfly Room*

Watson rushes through the house searching.

WATSON   There's someone in here. I can hear a movement.

Holmes kicks open the door.

Watson, gun in hand, rushes inside.

Beryl is tied to a pillar, muffled with towels and sheets.

Watson rapidly frees her.

HOLMES   Extraordinary. His butterfly collection. It is a museum in itself.

WATSON   The brute! Here, your brandy bottle!

Watson helps *Beryl* revive.

WATSON   She has fainted from ill-usage and exhaustion.

BERYL   Is he safe? Has he escaped?

HOLMES   He cannot escape us, madam.

BERYL   No, no, I did not mean my husband. Sir Henry? Is he safe? Stop that villain! See how he has treated me!

Beryl holds out her injured arms.

WATSON   What was that?

They listen in horror to the cry of the **Hound of the Baskervilles***.*

Scene 25: *The Hound of the Baskervilles*

The group members peer through the fog.

MICAH	Did you hear something?
ALI	I can't see anything.
DEVON	This fog.
VIC	Quiet!

Ali kneels and puts an ear to the ground.

ALI	I think I hear him coming.

Quick steps sound.

The group members crouch among the stones.

Henry emerges from the fog, glancing uneasily over his shoulders.

Henry passes on into the fog again.

ALI	Now what?
RAZ	Hist!
BROOK	Hist?
MICAH	Listen, idiot.
BROOK	Idiot, I'm not –
RAZ	OH
VIC	MY
DEVON	GOD

They freeze in horror.

*The **Hound of the Baskervilles** leaps past. (Is it a shadow, a construction, a masked or costumed actor? Whatever, the sense of terror is more important than – potentially comic – dogginess).*

RAZ	A hound it was.
ALI	An enormous coal-black hound.
MICAH	But not such a hound as mortal eyes have ever seen.
VIC	Fire burst from its open mouth.
BROOK	Its eyes glowed with a smouldering glare.
DEVON	Its muzzle and hackles and dewlap were outlined in flickering flame.

A gunshot.

A hideous howl.

***Holmes** and **Watson** rush past with **Beryl** – the group members follow them.*

***Henry** screams in the fog.*

Five more gunshots.

A last howl of agony.

*The fog lifts to reveal **Henry** unconscious and the dead **Hound** beside him.*

***Watson** presses his pistol to the **Hound**'s head.*

*Group members revive **Henry** with brandy.*

HENRY	My God! What was it? What, in heaven's name, was it?

HOLMES	It's dead, whatever it is. We have laid the family ghost once and forever.

Watson looks at the Hound's corpse.

WATSON	It is as large as a small lioness. Even dead those huge jaws seem to be dripping with a bluish flame.

Watson touches the Hound and holds up his fingers. They smoulder and glow.

WATSON	Phosphorus?
HOLMES	Or a cunning preparation of barium sulphide? We owe you a deep apology, Sir Henry, for having exposed you to this fright. I was prepared for a hound, but not for such a creature as this.
HENRY	You have saved my life.
HOLMES	Having first endangered it. There seemed no alternative but to catch him red-handed, and to do so we had to use you, alone, and apparently unprotected, as a bait.
HENRY	Catch him? Who?
BERYL	My husband. I have been his dupe and his tool.
HOLMES	The Stapletons being your disguised cousin Rodger Baskerville and his wife.
BERYL	I knew what he intended tonight. I told him I would not be an accessory to murder.
HOLMES	The lady tried to warn you once before, with the letter cut from *The Times*. So he trapped her in his butterfly collection.

WATSON	And who knows what his intentions were after this murderous night.
HOLMES	Tell us then where we shall find him. If you have ever aided him in evil, help us now and so atone.
BERYL	There is an old tin mine on an island in the heart of the mire. It was there that he kept his hound.

Holmes holds up a light.

WATSON	The fog lies like white wool.
HOLMES	No one could find his way into the Grimpen Mire tonight.

Beryl laughs.

| BERYL | He may find his way in, but never out. We planted guiding wands together, he and I, to mark the pathway through the mire. How can he see them now to escape? |

Holmes and Watson support Beryl and Henry off.

Scene 26: *Going Home*

Bright morning.

The group members, no longer playing their roles, pack up their tent.

DEVON	Hurry up.
VIC	We'll miss the train.
DEVON	Stuck here another night.
ALI	Wait.
BROOK	Careful!

Ali, supported by others, reaches deep into the mud and pulls out an old black boot.

ALI	Sir Henry's missing boot.
MICAH	Used to set the hound on his track.
VIC	Thrown away when the game was up.

Holmes enters.

Holmes shakes Watson's hand. (All the Watsons maybe?)

HOLMES	I say it again, Watson [and Watson, and Watson...] never yet have we helped to hunt down a more dangerous man than he who is lying yonder.

They all look across the moor for the last time.

Raz reads.

Raz 'Somewhere in the heart of the great Grimpen Mire, down in the foul slime of the huge morass which had sucked him in, this cold and cruel-hearted man is forever buried.'

The book is closed.

END

There are free resources available online to support the performance of this play. There is also a wealth of material on the themes and issues in the play and the life and times of Arthur Conan Doyle. Please visit **www.collinseducation.com/drama**